Let's Bake

# Thanksgiving Treats!

By Ruth Owen

Gareth Stevens
PUBLISHING

Published in 2018 by Gareth Stevens Publishing, 111 East 14th Street, Suite 349, New York, NY 10003

First Edition

Produced for Gareth Stevens Publishing by Ruby Tuesday Books Ltd
Designers: Tammy West and Emma Randall

Photo Credits:
Courtesy of Ruby Tuesday Books and Shutterstock.
Page 4 (center) courtesy of Alamy.


Cataloging-in-Publication Data
Names: Owen, Ruth.
Title: Let's bake Thanksgiving treats! / Ruth Owen.
Description: New York : Gareth Stevens Publishing, 2018. | Series: Holiday baking party | Includes index.
Identifiers: LCCN ISBN 9781538213407 (pbk.) | ISBN 9781538213421 (library bound) | ISBN 9781538213414 (6 pack)
Subjects: LCSH: Thanksgiving cooking--Juvenile literature. | Desserts--Juvenile literature.
Classification: LCC TX739.2.T45 O94 2018 | DDC 641.5'68--dc23


Manufactured in the United States of America

CPSIA compliance information: Batch #CW18GS: For further information contact Gareth Stevens, New York, New York at 1-800-542-2595.

# Contents

# Let's Get Baking!

It's the time of year for giving thanks and getting together with the friends and family we love. It's also a time for feasting on lots of seasonal goodies!

This year, show the people you love how thankful you are to have them in your life by baking them lots of sweet treats. Along with some key baking ingredients such as flour, butter, sugar, and eggs, you'll be getting creative with chocolate, pumpkin, cranberries, and seeds. So get your friends involved in the fun, too. Let's have a holiday baking party!

## Get Ready to Bake

- Before cooking, always wash your hands well with soap and hot water.
- Make sure the kitchen countertop and all your equipment is clean.
- Read the recipe carefully before you start cooking. If you don't understand a step, ask an adult to help you.
- Gather together all the ingredients and equipment you will need. Baking is more fun when you're prepared!

## Measuring Counts

Measuring cup

Measuring spoons

- Make sure you measure your ingredients carefully. If you get a measurement wrong, it could affect how successful your baking is.
  - Use measuring scales or a measuring cup to measure dry and liquid ingredients.
  - Measuring spoons can be used to measure small amounts of ingredients.

## Have Fun, Stay Safe!

It's very important to have an adult around whenever you do any of the following tasks in the kitchen:

- Using a mixer, the stovetop burners, or an oven.
- Using sharp utensils, such as knives and vegetable peelers or corers.
- Working with heated pans, pots, or baking sheets. Always use oven mitts when handling heated pans, pots, or baking sheets.

When you've finished baking, ALWAYS clean up the kitchen and put all your equipment away.

## Ingredients:

**To make the cookie dough:**
- 1 ½ cups all-purpose flour (plus a little extra for dusting)
- ½ cup superfine sugar
- 5 ounces butter or margarine (plus a little for greasing)

**For the frosting:**
- Fondant in fall colors
- Powdered sugar

## Equipment:
- 2 large cookie sheets
- Mixing bowl
- Wooden spoon
- Plastic wrap
- Rolling pin
- Leaf-shaped cookie cutters (Note: It's possible to buy leaf-shaped cookie cutters with veins. Alternatively, you can draw veins with the end of a wooden skewer.)
- Wooden skewer (optional)
- Oven mitts
- 2 potholders
- Wire rack for cooling

# Fall Leaf Cookies

These easy-to-make, leaf-shaped cookies are the perfect way to celebrate the beautiful colors of fall. The cookies are simply decorated with ready-to-roll frosting. So get your Thanksgiving baking party underway by making a batch of delicious fall leaf cookies in greens, oranges, and golds.

# Step 1
Grease the cookie sheets with a little butter to keep your cookies from sticking to the sheets.

# Step 2
Put the butter and sugar into the mixing bowl and **cream together** with the wooden spoon until smooth and fluffy.

# Step 3
Add the flour and mix the ingredients with the spoon. Next, use your hands to rub and combine the ingredients until the mixture looks like breadcrumbs.

Breadcrumb-like mixture

Flour

Creamed butter and sugar

Finally, use your hands to squeeze and **knead** the mixture to make a ball of soft dough.

# Step 4
Wrap the dough in plastic wrap and place in a refrigerator for 30 minutes.

# Step 5 **Preheat** the oven to 350°F (180°C).

Dough

# Step 6 Dust your countertop with a little flour. Unwrap the dough and place on the dusted surface. Use a rolling pin to roll out the dough to about ¼ inch (6 mm) thick.

# Step 7 Cut leaf shapes from the dough. Keep gathering up the spare dough and re-rolling it to make as many cookies as possible. Place the leaf cookies on the cookie sheets.

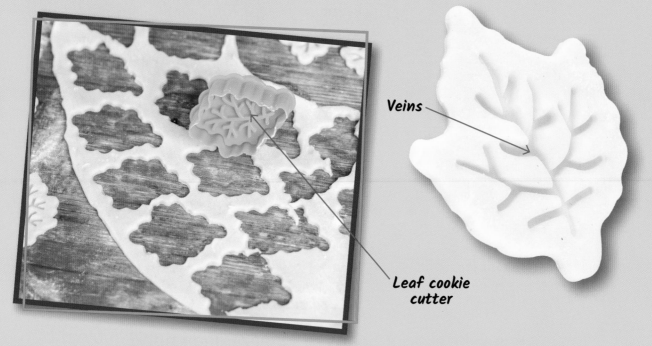

Veins

Leaf cookie cutter

# Step 8 Bake the cookies for about 15 minutes, or until they are turning golden. The centers of the cookies will still be slightly soft, but they'll soon firm up.

**Step 9** Remove the cookie sheets from the oven with oven mitts and stand the sheets on the potholders. Allow the cookies to cool for about 10 minutes, and then carefully place each cookie on a wire rack and allow to cool completely.

*You can simply dust the baked cookies with some powdered sugar.*

**Step 10** Dust your countertop with a little powdered sugar. Take a small lump of fondant and roll out to about ¼ inch (6 mm) thick. Cut a leaf shape from the frosting for each cookie.

**Step 11** Place a frosting leaf on top of each cookie and smooth down the edges.

Your delicious fall leaf cookies are ready to eat!

# Caramel, Cranberry, and Pumpkin Seed Bars

Pumpkins and cranberries have important roles to play in our Thanksgiving feasts. In this recipe, red cranberries and green pumpkin seeds are combined with creamy caramel to turn a simple homemade snack mix into a scrumptious holiday treat.

## Ingredients:

**To make the bars:**
- 9 ounces salted butter (plus a little extra for greasing)
- 14-ounce container of ready-to-use caramel
- ⅓ cup superfine sugar
- 3 ½ cups rolled oats
- ¾ cup cake flour

**To make the topping:**
- 2 ounces butter
- Leftover caramel from the can above
- ½ cup pumpkin seeds
- ½ cup dried cranberries
- ½ cup chocolate chips

## Equipment:
- 11 by 8 inch (28 x 20 cm) baking pan
- 2 saucepans
- Tablespoon
- Wooden spoon
- Mixing bowl
- Oven mitts
- Potholder
- Knife

# Step 1
Preheat the oven to 320°F (160°C).

# Step 2
Grease the baking pan with a little butter to keep the bars from sticking to the pan.

# Step 3
To make the bars, place the butter, sugar, and six tablespoons of caramel into a large saucepan.

Ready-to-use caramel

Superfine sugar

Butter

# Step 4
Heat over a medium heat, stirring occasionally, until the butter has melted.

# Step 5
Put the rolled oats and flour into a mixing bowl. Pour in the caramel mixture and stir until all the ingredients are combined.

Rolled oats

Cake flour

Snack bar mixture

**Step 6** Scoop the snack bar mixture into the baking pan. Press the mixture firmly into the pan with a spoon.

**Step 7** Bake the mixture for 30 to 35 minutes.

**Step 8** Remove the baking pan from the oven with oven mitts and stand on a potholder.

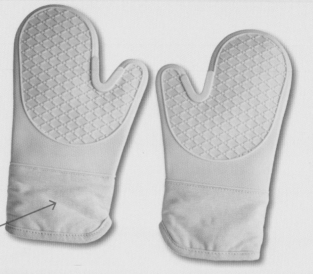

*Oven mitts*

**Step 9** To make the topping, put the butter and the remaining caramel into a saucepan. Heat on a medium heat, stirring occasionally, until the butter has melted and the mixture is smooth.

**Step 10** Pour the caramel topping over the baked snack bar mixture and allow to cool for about five minutes.

# Step 11

Sprinkle the cranberries, pumpkin seeds, and chocolate chips over the caramel topping.

*Cranberries, pumpkin seeds, and chocolate chips*

# Step 12

Leave to finish cooling and then put into the refrigerator overnight.

Cut into small squares to serve.

## Ingredients:

- 4 ounces butter (plus a little extra for greasing)
- 6 ounces of bittersweet chocolate
- Water
- 1 ½ cups superfine sugar
- 4 large eggs
- 1 tablespoon vanilla extract
- 2 cups all-purpose flour
- 1 teaspoon baking powder
- ½ teaspoon salt
- 1 ¼ cups canned pumpkin
- ¼ cup vegetable oil
- 1 teaspoon ground cinnamon
- ¼ teaspoon ground nutmeg

## Equipment:

- 11 by 8 inch (28 x 20 cm) baking pan
- Small saucepan
- Small heatproof bowl
- Wooden spoon
- Large mixing bowl
- Electric mixer (optional)
- Two medium mixing bowls
- Rubber spatula
- Oven mitts
- Potholder
- Knife

# Pumpkin Swirl Brownies

What could be nicer than a gooey, chocolaty brownie? A chocolate brownie swirled with pumpkin and spices! Not only do these brownies taste great, but their rich brown and bright orange colors are just perfect for Thanksgiving.

# Step 1
Grease the baking pan with a little butter to keep your brownies from sticking to the pan.

# Step 2
Preheat the oven to 350°F (180°C).

*Baking pan*

*Bittersweet chocolate*

# Step 3
Break the chocolate into small pieces and put in a heatproof bowl with the butter. Add about 1 inch (2.5 cm) of water to a small saucepan and stand the bowl in the saucepan. Heat the saucepan on a medium heat. As the water heats up it will melt the butter and chocolate. Keep stirring until the chocolate and butter are melted.

# Step 4
Put the sugar, eggs, and vanilla extract in the large mixing bowl. **Beat** the mixture with a wooden spoon until the ingredients are combined and fluffy. If you wish, you can use an electric mixer for steps 4 and 5.

# step 5
Add the flour, baking powder, and salt to the mixture in the bowl and beat until you have a thick, smooth batter.

*Batter*

# step 6
Divide the batter mixture between the two medium bowls.

*Canned pumpkin*

# step 7
Add the pumpkin, vegetable oil, cinnamon, and nutmeg to one of the medium bowls. Gently mix until well combined.

*Pumpkin batter*

# step 8
Add the melted chocolate and butter mixture to the second medium bowl. Gently mix until well combined.

*Chocolate batter*

# step 9
Pour about half the chocolate batter into the baking pan and smooth out with the spatula.

# Step 10
Next, pour about half the pumpkin batter on top of the chocolate layer and smooth out. Finally, pour on the remaining chocolate batter, followed by the remaining pumpkin batter.

# Step 11
With the rubber spatula gently swirl the batters to create a marbled effect.

# Step 12
Bake for 35 minutes. Use oven mitts to remove the pan from the oven. Stand the pan on a potholder and allow to cool completely.

*Swirled batter*

*Baked brownies*

Cut into squares and enjoy!

The quantities on this page will make 12 cupcakes.

## Ingredients:

**To make the cupcake batter:**
- 7 ounces butter or margarine
- 1 cup superfine sugar
- 2 cups cake flour
- 1 teaspoon baking powder
- ¼ teaspoon salt
- 3 large eggs
- ½ cup milk
- ½ teaspoon vanilla extract

**For the decorations and frosting:**
- 2 ½ cups powdered sugar
- ⅔ cup butter
- ⅔ cup peanut butter
- 2 teaspoons vanilla extract
- 4 tablespoons milk
- Assorted candies in yellow, orange, brown, red, or green

## Equipment:
- 12-hole muffin pan
- 12 muffin cases
- Mixing bowl
- Wooden spoon
- Electric mixer (optional)
- Oven mitt
- Metal skewer
- Potholder
- Small bowl
- Sieve
- Spoon
- Frosting gun

# Thanksgiving Cupcakes

Cupcakes are fun to make and delicious to eat. And with plenty of delicious peanut butter frosting and decorations in fall colors, these Thanksgiving cupcakes will make the perfect addition to your holiday celebrations.

**Step 1** Preheat the oven to 350°F (180°C).

**Step 2** Line the muffin pan with muffin cases.

Muffin pan

Muffin cases

**Step 3** Put the butter and sugar into the mixing bowl and cream together with a wooden spoon until fluffy. If you wish, you can do this step using an electric mixer.

**Step 4** Add the flour, baking powder, salt, eggs, milk, and vanilla extract to the bowl. Use a wooden spoon or electric mixer to beat the ingredients together until the mixture is thick and smooth.

**Step 5** Spoon the mixture into the muffin cases, sharing it equally.

Cupcake batter

**Step 6** Bake the cakes for 20 minutes, or until they have risen above the edges of the muffin cases. Using an oven mitt, remove the muffin pan from the oven. To test if the cakes are baked, insert a metal skewer into one cake. If it comes out clean, the cakes are ready.

**Step 7** Stand the muffin pan on a potholder and allow the cakes to cool completely.

## Step 8

To make the frosting, use the sieve to sift the powdered sugar into a small bowl. Add the butter, peanut butter, vanilla extract, and milk and mix until thick and smooth.

*Peanut butter*

## Step 9

Carefully spoon the frosting into a frosting gun. Gently create a swirled effect on the top of each cake. You can also spoon the frosting onto each cake and swirl with the back of the spoon to cover the top of the cake.

## Step 10

Decorate the frosting with colorful candies.

## Ingredients:

**To make the cookie dough:**
- 1 ½ cups all-purpose flour (plus a little extra for dusting)
- ½ cup superfine sugar
- 5 ounces butter or margarine (plus a little for greasing)
- 1 tablespoon vanilla extract

**For the frosting:**
- 1 cup powdered sugar
- 1 cup water
- Gel food coloring in your choice of colors
- Frosting tubes or pens

## Equipment:
- 2 large cookie sheets
- Mixing bowl
- Wooden spoon
- Plastic wrap
- A piece of clean cardboard
- A pencil and scissors
- Rolling pin
- A small knife
- Oven mitts
- 2 potholders
- Wire rack for cooling
- Sieve
- Small bowls
- Spoon (for mixing frosting)

# Turkey Cookies

This next recipe shows you how to bake up some cookies that will make your friends and family smile. Using your hand as a **template**, you can turn some sweet, buttery cookie dough into a batch of colorful, turkey-shaped treats. And nothing says Thanksgiving like a turkey!

Happy Thanksgiving

# Step 1
Grease the cookie sheets with a little butter to keep your cookies from sticking to the sheets.

**Superfine sugar**

**Butter**

# Step 2
Put the butter and sugar into the mixing bowl and cream together with the wooden spoon until smooth and fluffy.

Creamed butter and sugar

# Step 3
Add the flour and vanilla extract and mix the ingredients with the spoon. Next, use your hands to rub and combine the ingredients until the mixture looks like breadcrumbs.

Finally, use your hands to squeeze and knead the mixture to make a ball of soft dough.

**Cake flour**

**Vanilla extract**

Pure Vanilla Extract

Cookie dough

23

## Step 4
Wrap the dough in plastic wrap and place in a refrigerator for 30 minutes.

## Step 5
Preheat the oven to 350°F (180°C).

## Step 6
Place your hand on a piece of clean cardboard. Draw around your hand and then cut out the hand shape.

## Step 7
Dust your countertop with a little flour. Unwrap the dough and place on the dusted surface. Use a rolling pin to roll out the dough to about ¼ inch (6 mm) thick.

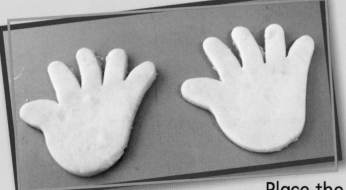

## Step 8
Place your cardboard hand shape on the dough and carefully cut around it with a small knife. Place the hand-shaped cookie on a cookie sheet. Cut more hand shapes and gather up any spare dough and re-roll it to make as many cookies as possible.

# Step 9
Bake the cookies for about 15 minutes, or until they are turning golden. The centers of the cookies will still be slightly soft, but they'll soon firm up.

# Step 10
Remove the cookie sheets from the oven with oven mitts and stand the sheets on the potholders. Allow the cookies to cool for about 10 minutes, and then carefully place each cookie on a wire rack and allow to cool completely.

# Step 11
Use the sieve to sift the powdered sugar into a small bowl. Little by little, add water and mix to make a simple, white frosting. The frosting should form a thick, spreadable **paste**.

Simple white frosting

# Step 12
To make colored frosting, put a little of the frosting into a separate bowl. Add a tiny blob of gel coloring. Mix and then add more coloring as needed to obtain the color you want.

Gel colorings

Yellow frosting

# Step 13
Finally, have fun decorating your turkey cookies with your homemade frosting or with colors from frosting tubes or pens.

# Mini Pumpkin Pies

## Ingredients:

**To make the pastry:**

- 4 cups all-purpose flour (plus extra for dusting)
- 8 ounces butter (plus a little extra for greasing)
- 1 cup superfine sugar
- 2 large eggs

**To make the filling:**

- 3 eggs
- 8 ounces softened cream cheese
- ½ cup superfine sugar
- 1 cup canned pumpkin
- 2 teaspoons vanilla extract
- 1 teaspoon pumpkin pie spice
- 1 teaspoon ground cinnamon

## Equipment:

- 1 12-hole or 2 6-hole muffin pans
- 2 mixing bowls
- Wooden spoon
- Plastic wrap
- Small bowl
- Hand whisk or electric mixer
- Rolling pin
- 4-inch (10-cm) round cutter
- Brush
- Spoon
- Oven mitts
- Potholders

Pumpkin pie is a **traditional** dessert at Thanksgiving. Instead of making one big pie for your Thanksgiving dinner, try baking these cute individual mini pumpkin pies. Serve them sprinkled with goodies such as toasted pumpkin seeds or pecan nuts, and of course a big dollop of whipped cream!

**Step 1** Grease the muffin pan with a little butter to keep your pies from sticking to the pan.

**Step 2** To make the pastry, put the butter and flour into a mixing bowl. Use your fingers to **rub in** the butter and flour until the mixture looks like breadcrumbs.

**Step 3** Stir in the sugar and eggs to the breadcrumb mixture.

**Step 4** Use your hands to gently combine and knead the mixture to make a ball of soft dough. The mixture will be very soft and crumbly.

**Step 5** Wrap the dough in plastic wrap and put in the refrigerator for about 20 minutes.

**Step 6** To make the pumpkin pie filling, separate one of the eggs and set the egg white to one side in a small bowl. Put the egg yolk and remaining two eggs into a mixing bowl.

# Step 7

Add the cream cheese, sugar, canned pumpkin, vanilla extract, pumpkin pie spice, and cinnamon to the eggs. Use a hand whisk or electric mixer to beat the ingredients until they form a thick, smooth mixture.

# Step 8

Preheat the oven to 350°F (180°C).

# Step 9

Dust your countertop with lots of flour. Unwrap the dough and place on the dusted surface. Use a rolling pin to roll out the dough to about ¼ inch (6 mm) thick.

Don't worry if the dough is very soft. It may be a little tricky to roll out, but persevere because the baked pie crusts will be beautifully soft and crumbly.

# Step 10

Cut circles from the dough and press into the muffin pan sections. If you don't have a large enough cutter, you can use the rim of a teacup or small bowl.

**Step 11** With a brush, whisk up the egg white you put to one side. Brush the edges of the pastry cases with the egg.

**Step 12** Spoon the pumpkin pie filling into the pastry cases, filling each pie almost to the top.

**Step 13** Bake the pies for up to 30 minutes. The pastry should turn a golden brown and the filling will be firm to the touch.

**Step 14** Remove the muffin pans from the oven with oven mitts and stand them on potholders. Allow the pies to cool a little before serving.

# Glossary

### beat
To blend a mixture of ingredients until they are smooth with equipment such as a spoon, fork, hand whisk, or electric mixer.

### cream together
To beat butter or margarine, usually with sugar, to make it light and fluffy.

### knead
To press, squeeze, and fold dough with your hands to make it smooth and stretchy.

### paste
A thick, soft, moist substance that can be stirred or spread. A paste is usually made by mixing dry ingredients with a small amount of liquid.

### preheat
To turn on an oven so it is at the correct temperature for cooking a particular dish before the food is placed inside.

### rub in

To use the fingers to rub flour (or other dry ingredients) into a fat, such as butter. This technique creates a breadcrumb-like mixture that is used to make pastry, crumbles, or scones.

### template

A shaped piece of a material such as cardboard that is used as a pattern for cutting out.

### traditional

Something that has been a custom, belief, or practice for a long time and has been passed on from one generation to the next.

# Index

# Further Information

Steele, Victoria. *101 Quick & Easy Cupcake and Muffin Recipes*.
CreateSpace Independent Publishing Platform, 2014.

Learn more about Thanksgiving here!
https://www.dkfindout.com/us/more-find-out/festivals-and-holidays/
thanksgiving/